A CATALONIAN CHRISTMAS CAROL
El Noi de la Mare

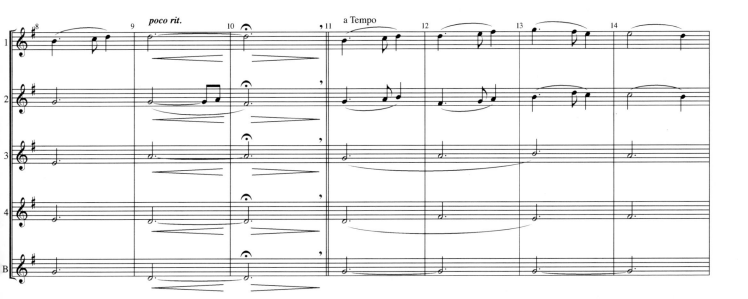

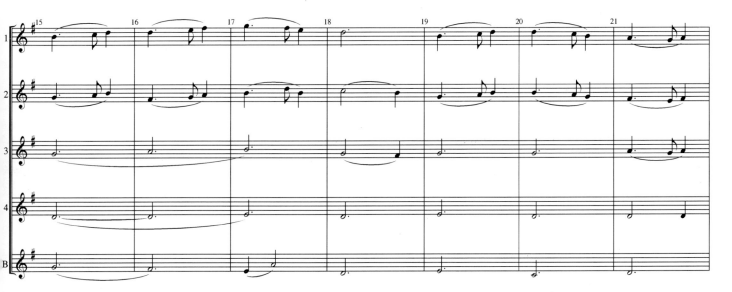

A CATALONIAN CHRISTMAS CAROL pg. 2

B♭ Clarinet 1

A CATALONIAN CHRISTMAS CAROL
El Noi de la Mare

Traditional Spanish Carol
Arranged by David Marlatt

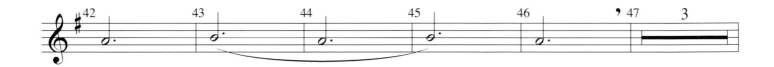

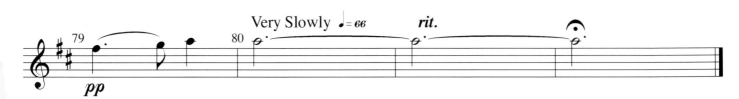

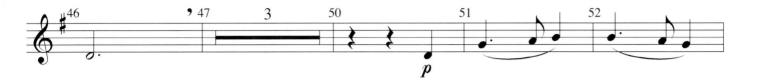

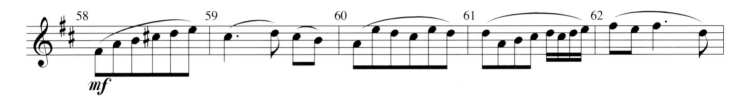

A CATALONIAN CHRISTMAS CAROL pg. 2

Bb Clarinet 2

A CATALONIAN CHRISTMAS CAROL
El Noi de la Mare

Traditional Spanish Carol
Arranged by David Marlatt

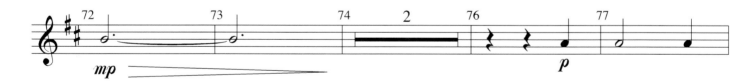

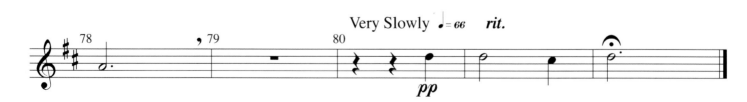

A CATALONIAN CHRISTMAS CAROL pg. 2

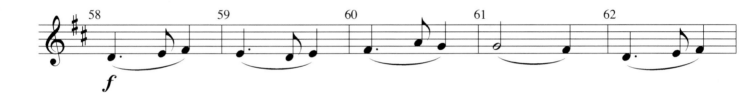

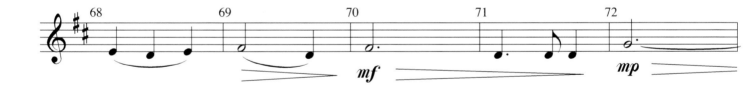

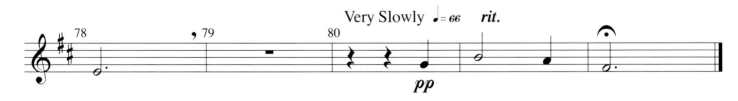

A CATALONIAN CHRISTMAS CAROL pg. 2

B♭ Bass Clarinet

A CATALONIAN CHRISTMAS CAROL
El Noi de la Mare

Traditional Spanish Carol
Arranged by David Marlatt

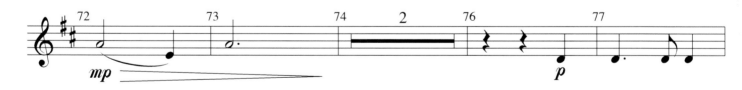

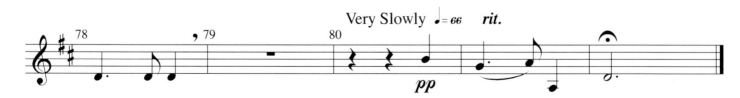

A CATALONIAN CHRISTMAS CAROL pg. 2

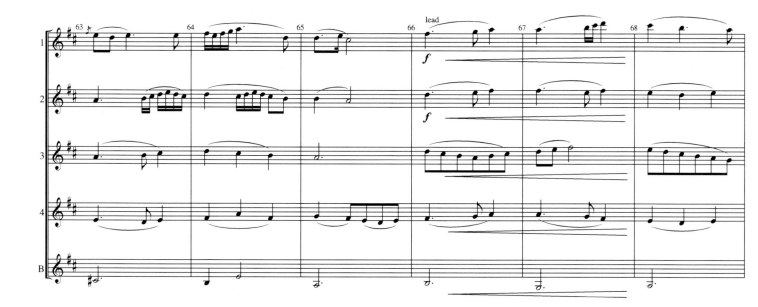

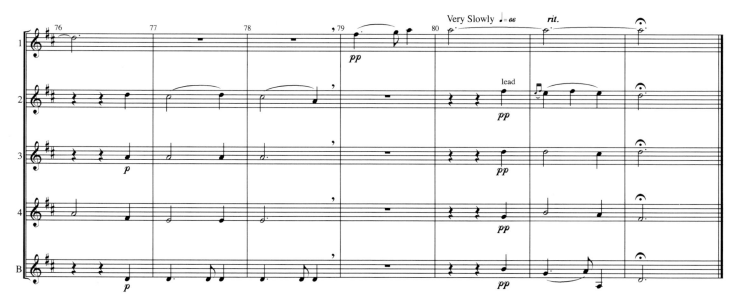